The more I see
of men

the more I love
my dog

Olivia Edward
Illustrations by Alex Hallatt

summersdale

THE MORE I SEE OF MEN, THE MORE I LOVE MY DOG

First published in 2002
Reprinted 2003, 2004, 2005, 2006 and 2009
This edition copyright © Summersdale Publishers Ltd, 2013

Illustrations by Alex Hallatt

Summersdale Publishers Ltd
46 West Street
Chichester
West Sussex
PO19 1RP
UK

www.summersdale.com

Printed and bound in China

ISBN: 978-1-84953-404-8

Substantial discounts on bulk quantities of Summersdale books are available to corporations, professional associations and other organisations. For details contact Nicky Douglas by telephone: +44 (0) 1243-756902, fax: +44 (0) 1243-786300 or email: nicky@summersdale.com.

For SPF and Thistle

Introduction

Dogs are better than men. They are much cheaper and more easily replaceable. They won't help around the house, but a cute, well-chosen woofer will open up a whole world of social possibilities. When was the last time someone engaged you in conversation by pointing at your partner and saying, 'Ah, that's a fine-looking beast you've got there. Can I stroke him?'

Not yet convinced? You'll be sure to change your mind after reading the following reasons why a furry four-pawed companion is far superior to a flabby flat-footed man.

Dogs are always
delighted that you
have graced them with
your company.

Dogs don't come home
angry and stressed
after a hard day
in the park.

Dogs miss you when you are gone.

You don't need
to spend hours
wondering where your
relationship with your
dog is going.

Cute dogs don't know
they are cute.

Dogs are not excited
by a large pair of
unfamiliar breasts.

Irritating dogs can
be plonked outside
when you need some
personal space.

Dogs won't help
themselves to
your cash.

You can leave a dog at home when you want a wild night out... and your dog won't quiz you when you come in drunk at 3 a.m. with torn tights.

Dogs feel guilty and are visibly remorseful when they have done something wrong.

It is highly unlikely
that you will be seized
by an overwhelming
desire to take your
best friend's dog home
for the night.

Dogs understand when you are snappy, and respond accordingly by offering more affection.

Dogs are not
embarrassed about
expressing their
affection for you
in public.

You never
look at your
dog and wonder
whether you still
love them.

Dogs don't need
constant reassurance
that you find them
more appealing than
dogs on TV, the dog
next door, dogs at
work, or your best
friend's dog.

Dogs don't think less of you for not being able to understand the intricacies of the rules of sports.

A dog will never criticise your driving (but most men won't try to sit on your lap when you're at the wheel of your car).

Dogs think that everything you feed them is delicious.

Dogs think with their stomachs. We all know what men think with.

Dogs may give other
women attention, but
they will always come
when they are called.

Dogs don't point
out when you
have spots.

Dogs know how
to listen.

A dog won't
complain about
your 'dull' friends.

Dogs don't think you are boring when you spend a night in front of the telly.

Dogs are always happy
to see your family.

Dogs don't feel
insecure because you
earn more money
than they do.

Dogs don't mind when
you put on weight.

Dogs make it very
clear if they want
to go out.

Dogs admit it when
they are jealous.

Dogs understand
the concepts of
commitment and
loyalty.

You just know
your dog is
The One.

Dogs are not ashamed
to admit they are lost.

You won't throw a strop and refuse to play with your dog because they always get too competitive.

Dogs don't change
the subject.

Dogs know exactly how to behave when you are watching an emotional film: to remain silent and cuddle affectionately without demanding sex or fidgeting.

Dogs don't snigger at your inability to throw overarm when you are playing fetch.

Dogs look you in the eye when you are speaking to them.

Dogs don't resent your
dominant position in
the relationship.

Dogs understand
that the correct way
to make up with
you is to be entirely
submissive whilst
strongly reaffirming
their love for you.

Your dog will continue to show the greatest respect for you, even if you destroy your car's engine by forgetting to top up the oil.

To sustain a relationship with your dog, it is not necessary to feign an interest in their hobbies.

Dogs don't complain when you are late. In fact, they are happier to see you than if you had been on time.

Dogs don't bring other loud, smelly dogs back to your house to watch the game.

Dogs sulk quietly in their beds. They do not draw attention to their unhappiness by huffing loudly and banging doors.

Dogs make it clear when they don't like other dogs. They don't mutter insults under their breath.

Dogs don't purchase flashy sports cars to prove they are still young dogs at heart.

A dog can be tied up
on shopping trips so
you know you won't
return to find them
browsing in the
hi-fi store.

Dogs don't go
bald in their
senior years.

Dogs can be
house-trained.

Excitable dogs can be
kept on tight leads in
public places.

Dogs don't feel
the need to prove
themselves by jumping
higher, running faster
or drinking more
water than other dogs.

Dogs know
that you are
always right.

Dogs don't wear embarrassing, unfashionable items of clothing – unless you want to dress them in a little red jacket and matching booties.

With a dog, you don't have to wait for the right time before announcing that your mother is coming to stay.

Dogs are not possessive about the TV remote control. They won't touch it unless you throw it across the room in anger. In which case they will bring it back to you.

Dogs don't pretend the dog they rushed up to in the park and leapt on with wild abandon was just a friend.

Your dog will not feign
knowledge of a subject
they know nothing
about in order to
impress other dogs.

Your dog won't run off
with your best friend...
unless you forget to
feed them.

Fat dogs can be put on
diets. They won't order
any sneaky kebabs
when they think you're
not looking.

If your dog smells
unpleasant or snores
in the night, you can
simply push them
out of bed.

If you're interested in finding out more about our humour books, follow us on Twitter: @Summersdale

www.summersdale.com